OCEANS

BY

MIKE CLARK

©2017
Book Life
King's Lynn
Norfolk PE30 4LS

ISBN: 978-1-78637-167-6

Written by:
Mike Clark

Edited by:
Charlie Ogden

Designed by:
Drue Rintoul

A catalogue record for this book
is available from the British Library.

Photocredits
Abbreviations: l-left, r-right, b-bottom, t-top, c-centre, m-middle.

Front Cover – Tischenko Irina. 1 – bluehand. 2 – stockphoto-graf. 4bl – MicheleBoiero. 4br – Frances van der Merwe. 5 – Paul B. Moore. 6 – PHOTOCREO Michal Bednarek. 8t – KARI K. 8b – photomatz. 9t – PIYAPONG THONGDUMHYU. 10t – Saran Poroong. 10b – gabriel12. 11t – Jon Sturgeon. 11b – Shams Ashraf. 12t – TravelMediaProductions. 12bl – alterfalter. 12br – Lebendkulturen.de. 13t – Jan Martin Will. 13m – Sylvie Bouchard. 13b – Vladimir Melnik. 14t – Ethan Daniels. 14bl – Jean-Edouard Rozey. 14br – NatalieJean. 15t – Kidd Silencer. 15b – Andrea Izzotti. 16-17 background – Andrey_Kuzmin. 16t – littlesam. 16b – Laura Dinraths. 17t – Luiz A. Rocha. 17b – stockpix4u. 18tl – Rui Manuel Teles Gomes. 18tr – Dmytro Pylypenko. 18b – Mohamed AlQubaisi. 19t – Krzysztof Odziomek. 19m – Andrea Izzotti. 19b – By D Ramey Logan (Own work) [CC BY-SA 3.0 (http://creativecommons.org/licenses/by-sa/3.0)], via Wikimedia Commons. 20tl – Greg Amptman. 20b – Digital Storm. 21tl – Lance Sagar. 21m – Potapov Alexander. 21b – Tory Kallman. 22t – © Citron / , via Wikimedia Commons. 22br – By Peter Southwood (Own work) [CC BY-SA 3.0 (http://creativecommons.org/licenses/by-sa/3.0)], via Wikimedia Commons. 23t – Javontaevious at English Wikipedia [GFDL (http://www.gnu.org/copyleft/fdl.html) or CC BY-SA 3.0 (http://creativecommons.org/licenses/by-sa/3.0)], via Wikimedia Commons. 23b – By NOAA Okeanos Explorer Program, Galapagos Rift Expedition 2011 (Flickr NOAA Photo Library) [Public domain], via Wikimedia Commons. 24t – best works. 24b – JC Photo. 25t – Ethan Daniels. 25b – BlueOrange Studio. 26t – Peter Hermes Furian. 26b – Giedriius. 26c – Anton Balazh . 27t – AndreAnita. 27b – Kjetil Kolbjornsrud. 27c – Anton Balazh. 28t – Rich Carey. 28b – buttchi 3 Sha Life. 29t – operafotografca. 29b – Photographee.eu.Images are courtesy of Shutterstock.com. With thanks to Getty Images, Thinkstock Photo and iStockphoto.

CONTENTS

Words in **bold** are explained in the glossary on page 31.

Habitats and Biomes

WHAT ARE HABITATS?

Habitats are places where plants and animals live. Habitats can include everything from mountains and rivers to deserts and oceans – even other living things!

The animals and plants that live in a habitat usually become **adapted** to it. This means that they become very good at raising their young and finding food and water in their specific habitat. A habitat can also give an animal protection from **predators**, often by having lots of places to hide. This helps animals to **reproduce** safely.

Mountain Goat

Mountain goats have great balance and can jump large distances from rock to rock. Up here it is safe, as predators cannot travel along the rocks as fast as the goats can.

Animals that only live on other living things are called parasites. Aphids are parasites because they live on plants and take food from the plants.

Aphid

WHAT IS A BIOME?

A biome is a very large area of the world where the **climate** is very similar. Because biomes are so huge, they usually contain many different habitats. As a biome's climate is the same all the way across it, often the animals and plants that live in the same biome will be very similar, even if they live in very different habitats. While some animals and plants are able to live in different habitats within the same biome, most living things can only live in one habitat.

For example, cactus plants can survive in dry deserts because they can store water. This helps them to survive long periods without rain. But in the rainforest, the cactus would not survive. Other plants would grow over the top of the cactus, blocking out the sunlight that the cactus needs to survive.

Some plants survive better in the dry, sunny conditions in the desert, whereas other plants survive better in the dark, damp conditions in the rainforest. This shows how living things adapt to their **environment**.

What Are Oceans?

Ocean biomes are huge areas of **saltwater**. There are five oceans in the world: the Arctic, Pacific, Atlantic, Indian and Southern Ocean. Together they make up over 70% of the Earth's surface.

All ocean habitats are broken up into three main areas. The first is coastal areas, which are the places where the ocean meets the land. The second is open ocean, which are areas near the surface of ocean that are exposed to sunlight. The final main area of the ocean is the deep sea, which lies far beneath the open ocean and doesn't receive any sunlight. Within these areas there are lots of different habitats, such as seashores, coral reefs, kelp forests and seagrass meadows.

Arctic Ocean

Atlantic Ocean

Pacific Ocean

Pacific Ocean

Indian Ocean

Southern Ocean

The ocean is also divided into layers. These layers break up the ocean by how much sunlight each layer gets. The layers near the surface of the water get more sunlight and the layers near the ocean floor get less sunlight.

The **water pressure** changes as you go deeper into the ocean. Deeper areas of the ocean have a much higher water pressure. This means that the animals that live near the surface of the ocean usually cannot swim all the way down to the deep ocean, because the higher water pressure would squash them!

Ocean biomes are often called **marine** biomes by scientists.

Sunlight Zone

Twilight Zone

Midnight Zone

Abyssal Zone

Ocean Habitats

Ocean habitats all contain saltwater instead of fresh water. When it rains, the rainwater washes the salt from the land into the ocean. Too much salt can kill many animals, but most animals that live in the ocean have become adapted to living in saltwater.

The ocean is home to many different types of animal. Most of these animals only live in small parts of the ocean, but some spend their lives travelling across entire ocean biomes.

Most of the animals in ocean biomes live in the upper layers of the ocean, such as the sunlight and twilight zones. This is where seaweed, seagrass, **phytoplankton** and other **photosynthesising** living things live. This is because all of these things need sunlight to make food.

Deeper areas of the ocean, such as the midnight and abyssal zones, have no sunlight. Animals that live in these parts of the ocean depend on the food that floats down from above. This can sometimes make finding food difficult for these animals, which is why many animals that live in the deep ocean have adapted to be able to go for months without food!

Phytoplankton

The bottom of the ocean can be as cold as -3 °C

Sunny Seashores

Plants and animals that live on the seashore like to live in shallow waters. One plant that often lives near the shore is seaweed. Many types of seaweed like to have something firm that they can attach themselves to, such as a big rock. They also need lots of water. Most seashores have both of these things all year round.

Many seashores have beaches made of sand. Sand is made up of very tiny rocks that have been broken up by the ocean. The ocean washes these tiny bits of rock onto the shore, creating beaches. The sand is the perfect place to hide for many animals. One such animal is the sand crab, which hides from predators by burying itself in the sand.

Sand Crab

Seaweed growing on rocks.

The seashore is also home to many birds. Gulls are one of the most common types of bird at the beach. When they're not stealing chips, they're **scavenging** for food on the rocks and sand, looking for crabs and other small sea creatures. They're also very good at fishing and can dive into the ocean to catch fish that are swimming near the surface.

A gull bringing a crab back to shore to eat.

One of the best fishers at the seashore is the pelican. This bird has adapted its beak into a very special tool for fishing. The lower part of its **bill** is like a big, stretchy bag. The pelican catches fish by skimming its bill along the surface of the ocean, scooping up fish and water. The pelican's special bill drains the water out before the fish are swallowed.

Some seabirds can stay in the air for over a month without needing to land.

Pelican

11

Icy Seashores

The seashores near the North and South Poles are very cold because they do not get much sunlight. There is only one type of bird that stays on these icy seashores all year round: the penguin. These birds cannot fly; instead, they have adapted to be fantastic swimmers.

Emperor penguins jumping out of the ocean.

Emperor penguins, which live in **Antarctica**, have adapted to have thick skin and a layer of **blubber** that helps to keep them warm. They mainly eat fish such as Antarctic silverfish and sardines. These fish are very small and feed on very tiny animals called copepods, which themselves eat plankton.

Copepod

Sardines

Emperor Penguins can dive up to 565 metres deep into the ocean and can stay underwater for more than 20 minutes.

In Antarctica, the emperor penguin is safe on land because there aren't any predators that hunt them there. In the sea, however, the penguins are not so safe. The biggest danger for penguins in Antarctica comes from leopard seals. These animals are slow on land but are very fast in the water.

Leopard Seal

Polar Bear

Not all animals on icy shores are good swimmers. The walrus, which can be found in the Arctic, is very heavy and a slow swimmer. But walruses don't need to be fast as they only eat **crustaceans**, which also move very slowly. Their thick skin protects their body from attacks from polar bears and their tusks are used as defensive weapons.

A male walrus' tusks can grow up to a metre long.

Walrus

13

Underwater Forests and Meadows

In shallow ocean waters, where there is a lot of sunlight, many kelp forests and seagrass meadows grow. A kelp forest is not made up of trees – it's actually made from seaweed. This seaweed grows long stems with many leaves that float up to the ocean surface for light.

Kelp forests are home to a wide range of animals. One of these animals is the sea otter. These otters catch all kinds of animals, including fish, crabs and even sea urchins. Sea urchins destroy the kelp and so, by eating them, the otters help to keep their habitat alive. The sea otters don't even need to go back to the shore to eat, they simply float on their back as they enjoy their food.

Kelp Forest

A sea otter trying to work out how to eat a crab.

Sea Urchin

Shallow waters are also home to seagrass meadows, which are the natural habitat of seahorses. Seahorses hide in the seagrass while hunting tiny crustaceans. The seagrass gives the seahorse something to hold on to with its tail, which stops the seahorse from being washed away by a strong **current**. This is a great example of how animals adapt to the plants in their habitat.

A seahorse holding onto seagrass with its tail.

Some animals that live in these habitats use the seagrass for food. The manatee, which is also called the sea cow, spends most of its day eating seagrass. The manatee can swim as fast as 30 kilometres an hour but, as it has no predators, they mostly just drift around very slowly.

West Indian Manatee

15

Coral Reefs

Coral reef habitats are found in ocean waters that are around 25 °C and are filled with creatures called coral. For many years, coral was believed to be a plant, but it is actually a **colony** of tiny animals called polyps. Corals grow on parts of the ocean floor that receive lots of sunlight and they mostly eat plankton that they catch in their tiny tentacles.

Also living in the coral are many types of starfish. Starfish mainly eat slow-growing things such as **algae** and even coral. If caught by a predator, the starfish will shed one of its own **limbs** to escape. The starfish will then regrow the lost limb over a few months.

Polyp

Branch

This is a close-up view of a coral's branches and the polyps.

The Great Barrier Reef is the world's largest coral reef and it stretches over 2,300 kilometres!

Pebble Red Seastar

Harlequin Shrimp

One of the starfish's main predators is the harlequin shrimp. This shrimp is only found in coral reefs and it mostly eats starfish. The shrimp's shell is very colourful and this helps the animal to blend in with the colourful corals.

Mandarinfish

The mandarinfish is also only found in coral reefs. The mandarinfish is one of the most colourful animals in the entire world, which helps it to hide in the colourful corals and not be seen. It mostly eats copepods, small fish eggs and other very small creatures that hide in the coral.

Open Ocean

The open ocean is very big and the creatures that live there spend most of their time very far apart from one another. There is no land below to hold on to; it drops down for hundreds of metres. Because of this, only tiny floating phytoplankton grow here. Phytoplankton are eaten by krill and types of zooplankton, which swim around in huge groups.

Krill and plankton are both very important to the **ecosystem** in the open ocean. They sit at the bottom of the **food chain** and are eaten by a range of different creatures, such as sardines, golden jellyfish and even baby squids. These animals are then eaten by bigger open ocean predators such as the ocean sunfish.

A close up image of a krill.

Ocean Sunfish

A swarm of golden jellyfish in Palau.

Whale Shark

Krill isn't just important to the diet of small fish. The whale shark, which is the largest fish in the ocean, swims along with its huge mouth wide open, collecting krill. Whale sharks are so peaceful that they even allow other fish to ride on their backs.

The largest krill-eater, and the largest animal in the world, is the blue whale. This whale has whisker-like teeth that are great at catching krill. These whales are so big that they are actually a habitat to other living things called whale barnacles. These small creatures grow on the whale's skin and eat plankton as the whale swims along.

Growing on this whale's skin is a group of whale barnacles.

An adult blue whale eats up to 40 million krill a day.

Blue Whale

19

Big Ocean Hunters

The open ocean contains many of the world's most amazing predators. One of the strangest is the lion's mane jellyfish. Most jellyfish are quite small, but this one grows to be over 2 metres wide and its tentacles can be up to 37 metres long! These tentacles are like a big net that catches fish and kills them with a sting before eating them.

The largest and most famous predator on Earth is the great white shark. The open ocean is so large that great white sharks have adapted to be able to sense the movements of fish from hundreds of metres away. This helps them to save their energy until there is something nearby to eat. The great white shark can also sense a drop of blood from thousands of metres away!

Lion's Mane Jellyfish

Many other sharks can sense blood in the ocean from 500 metres away!

Great White Shark

While most animals that live in the ocean are fish, there are also lots of mammals in the ocean. Mammals have to breathe air, which means that mammals that live in the ocean have to come to the surface to breathe. Many ocean mammals are pack hunters, meaning that they hunt in a large group called a pod. One of the world's greatest pack hunters is the dolphin. Dolphins work so well together that they can chase fish into a small space and take turns grabbing them.

A Pod of Spinner Dolphins

The rulers of the open ocean are killer whales. These mammals also hunt in groups. They are larger than great white sharks and hunt many different types of animal, including seals, sharks and even other whales!

Killer whales are also known as orcas.

Deep Sea

Deep down in the ocean there is very little light. It is so dark that it is very difficult to capture anything on camera. Luckily, many brave explorers, armed with sketch pads, have come back with drawings of the strange creatures that live down in the deep.

The deep sea has very little food and most creatures that live down there depend on what sinks down from the waters above for food. The vampire squid swims around the upper areas of the deep sea. It doesn't drink blood, as its name would have you believe. Instead, it catches tiny pieces of food that sink down from surface waters above. They do this by sending out a very thin tentacle that sticks to the tiny pieces.

Vampire Squid

The hagfish is one of the best scavengers on the sea floor. Not only can it take in food through its mouth, but it can also absorb tiny bits through its skin. The hagfish can also smell **decaying** food from many kilometres away. But large amounts of food don't come along often, so the hagfish has adapted to be able to live for months without food.

One of the scariest deep sea creatures has to be the anglerfish. Even though there are many different types of anglerfish, they are very hard to find. One reason for this, other than because they hide deep at the bottom of the ocean, is because they are small. Anglerfish only grow up

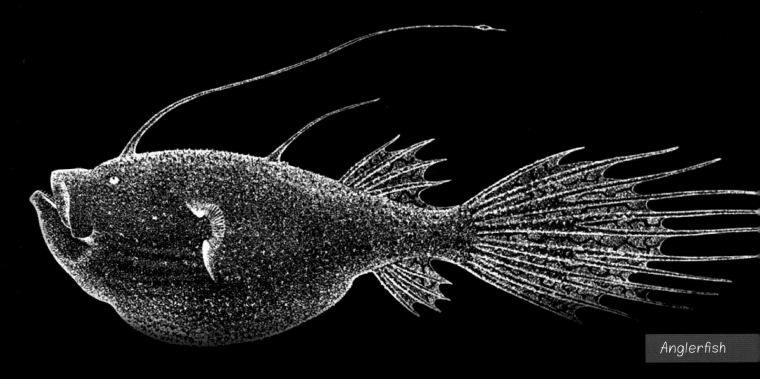

Anglerfish

Despite their size, these fish are great hunters and have adapted a very special tool for getting food. They have a worm-like **lure** that grows from the top of their head and glows in the darkness of the ocean. This light attracts very small prey, such as fish and shrimp, that believe it might be food. Once the prey comes close enough, the anglerfish will gobble them up.

This striated frogfish is a type of anglerfish.

Pacific Ocean

The Pacific Ocean is the biggest ocean in the world. It is also home to the deepest point in any ocean – the Mariana Trench. The whole of Mount Everest could fit inside the Mariana Trench and there would still be room to spare!

Mount Everest
8,848 metres high

Mariana Trench
10,911 metres deep

The Pacific Ocean is home to more coral reefs than any other ocean on the planet. It is also home to the world's largest coral reef – the Great Barrier Reef – which is off the coast of Australia.

The Great Barrier Reef

The Pacific Ocean is home to lots of different habitats. Unlike other oceans, the Pacific is home to warm beaches and it is filled with small islands that have shallow areas of water around them. These shallow areas of water provide the perfect conditions for kelp forests and seagrass meadows to grow.

Kelp Forest

Many of the fish that live in the Pacific Ocean can only live in these areas. These animals are very sensitive to heat and the depth of the ocean, so they cannot move to other areas of the Pacific Ocean.

Palau, a country in the Pacific Ocean, is made up of hundreds of islands. The waters around these islands are home to some incredible animals that can only be found near islands in the Pacific Ocean.

25

Arctic Ocean

The Arctic Ocean is the world's smallest ocean and it is also the most shallow. Its deepest point could only fit about half of Mount Everest inside of it. Most of the time, the ocean is covered in very large chunks of ice.

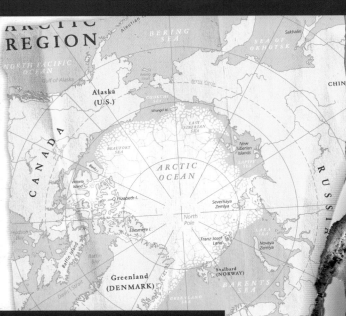

The white area on this map shows the area of the Arctic Ocean that is covered by ice.

The word Arctic comes from the Greek word for 'bear'. The Arctic Ocean got its name because a lot of the land around the Arctic Ocean is home to bears

Brown bears are just one type of bear that live near to the Arctic Ocean.

The animals that live in the Arctic have adapted to the extreme temperatures, which can be as cold as -30 °C. When temperatures get very cold, polar bears stay out of the cold winds by tunnelling under the snow.

A polar bear peeping out of its den.

The ocean is actually much warmer than the land around it, but at its warmest it still only gets to about -1 °C. Because of this, many animals that swim in warmer oceans can also swim in the Arctic Ocean. Fish such as cod and mammals such as humpback whales can be found in the Arctic Ocean as well as in other oceans, such as the Atlantic, Pacific and Indian oceans.

A humpback whale's tail as it dives below the surface of the Arctic Ocean.

Protecting the Oceans

Plastic Rubbish

Many ocean habitats are now under threat from **pollution**. The middle of the Atlantic Ocean is filled with huge amounts of plastic rubbish. This rubbish is very dangerous for the animals that live in the Atlantic Ocean. Many get caught in the plastic and others eat the plastic, which then gets stuck in their stomachs and often causes them to die.

As well as this, the gases that are given off by factories and cars also harm ocean habitats. These gases are causing the Earth and its oceans to get hotter and hotter. Because many of the animals that live in the ocean are sensitive to temperature, the slightest change in temperature could make it so that many animals can no longer live in their habitats. The coral of the Great Barrier Reef is very sensitive to changes in temperature and when it gets too hot, it cannot eat and starts to die.

Temperatures that are too warm also cause coral to turn white. Scientists call this 'coral bleaching'.

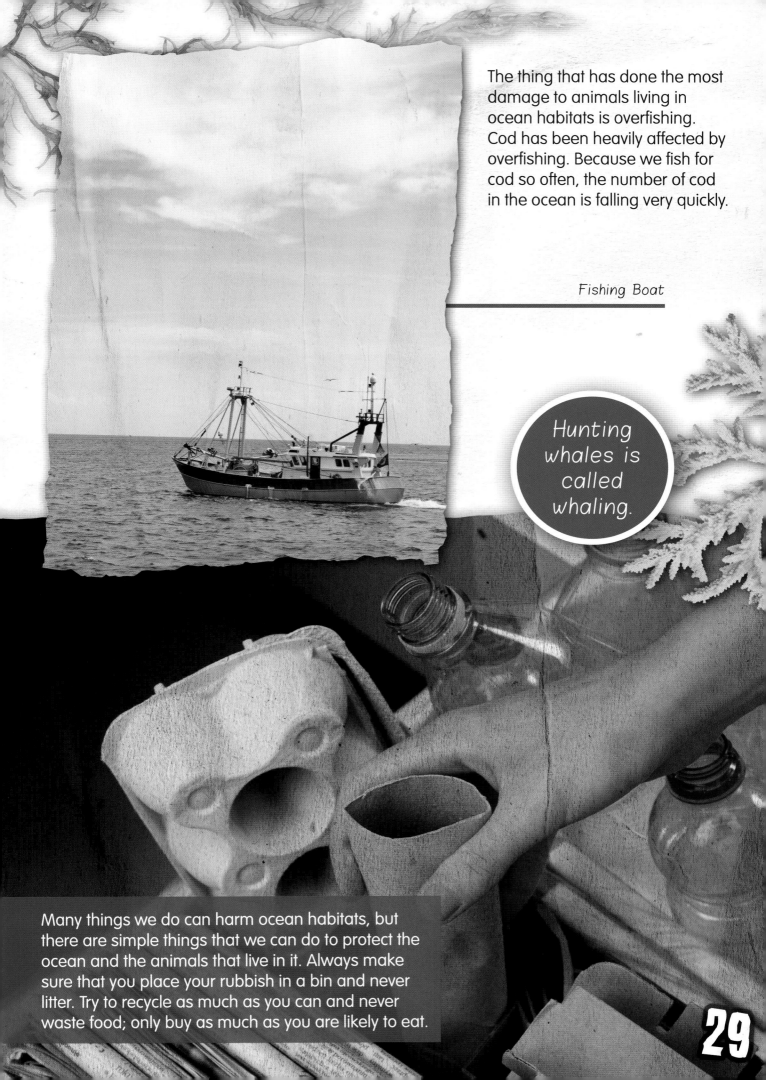

The thing that has done the most damage to animals living in ocean habitats is overfishing. Cod has been heavily affected by overfishing. Because we fish for cod so often, the number of cod in the ocean is falling very quickly.

Fishing Boat

Hunting whales is called whaling.

Many things we do can harm ocean habitats, but there are simple things that we can do to protect the ocean and the animals that live in it. Always make sure that you place your rubbish in a bin and never litter. Try to recycle as much as you can and never waste food; only buy as much as you are likely to eat.

Quick Quiz and Useful Links

Quick Quiz

Can you name all five oceans?

What type of water is in the ocean?

Where do leopard seals live?

Where do sea otters live?

What is the largest fish?

What do blue whales eat?

How do anglerfish catch their food?

What is the deepest point in the Pacific Ocean called?

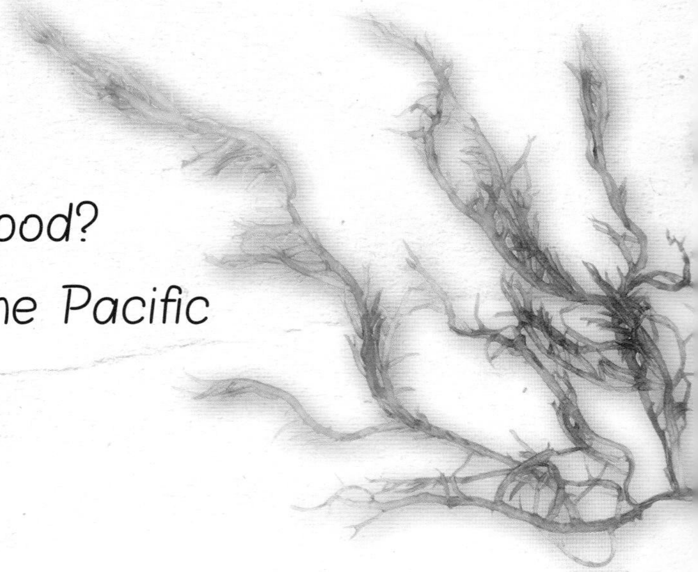

Useful Links

Check out these awesome websites for more facts about the ocean:

bbc.co.uk/nature/habitats

gowild.wwf.org.uk

ngkids.co.uk

Glossary

adapted	changed over time to suit different conditions
algae	living things that are like plants, but have no roots, stems, leaves or flowers
Antarctica	the continent surrounding the South Pole
bill	another name for the beak of some birds
blubber	a thick layer of fat under the skin of sea mammals, such as whales and seals
°C	a symbol meaning 'degrees Celsius'
climate	the common weather in a certain place
colony	a group of animals that live very close together
crustaceans	a type of animal that lives in water and has a hard outer shell
current	a steady flow of water in one direction
decaying	to rot or decompose
ecosystem	a group of interacting animals and plants and their physical environment
environment	natural world
food chain	a way of describing what eats what in an ecosystem
limbs	arms and legs, as well as the wings of birds
lure	a type of bait used to attract fish when hunting
marine	relating to the ocean
photosynthesising	a special way plants make food using sunlight, water and gases in the air
phytoplankton	very small plants that are barely visible to the naked eye
pollution	the act of introducing harmful or poisonous substances into an environment
predators	animals that hunt other animals for food
reproduce	to produce young through the act of mating
saltwater	water with a high amount of salt in it; sea or ocean water
scavenging	to feed on animals that are already dead
water pressure	the amount of force with which water pushes down on the things below it

Index